AQA GCSE ENGLISH LANGUAGE – PAPER 2: SECTION B: WRITING: 12 A STAR EXAM ANSWERS

Full mark A Star (Grade 9) Answers

By Joseph Anthony Campbell

First Printing: October 2023

CONTENTS

THE QUALITY CONTROL SYSTEM™ OR HOW TO GET AN A STAR!

The Quality Control System™ is fourfold.

It involves:

1) An efficient summary of the examination paper.

2) A concise focus upon the Assessment Objectives in the exam and how to approach them.

3) Clear instructions on your timings and how long you should spend on each question. *This is the most important point of fact in this fourfold system*.

4) Further to point 3, the approximate word count per minute you should be consistently aiming for in each minute of your exam.

My students have applied all of the techniques of the Quality Control System™ I am providing you with to gain A stars (Grade 9's) in their examinations. You can replicate them by following the advice in this book. Following these rules has ensured success for my students in English Language and their other subjects and it will do for you too! The Quality Control System is explained more fully at the end of this book.

AQA ENGLISH LANGUAGE GCSE – THE BEST APPROACH TO A GRADE 9!

From 2024 onwards you will be asked to write an 'Article', a 'Letter' or a 'Speech'.
There are examples of seven Grade 9 'Article' answers in this book.
There are examples of three Grade 9 'Letter' answers in this book.
There are examples of two Grade 9 'Speech' answers in this book.

The best approach for a Grade 9 is to spend 45 to 50 minutes on each question; 40 minutes writing and 10 minutes making notes, planning and checking your final answer for basic corrections at the end of the examination.

The following 12 questions and answers will help you to prepare your own Grade 9 essays and to massively improve your own practice for your exams. Although your questions will, of course, be different in your examination, the examples I have provided demonstrate clearly the techniques and linguistic devices expected by the AQA exam board in order to achieve a Grade 9.

This series of model answer books have helped thousands of readers to achieve their full potential!

PAPER 2: SECTION B: WRITING: FIRST ESSAY: NEWSPAPER ARTICLE

You are advised to spend about 45 to 50 minutes on this section.

Write in full sentences.

You are reminded of the need to plan your answer.

You should leave enough time to check your work at the end.

Question: *'Homework has no value. Some students get it done for them; some don't do it at all. Students should be relaxing in their free time.'*

Write an article for a broadsheet newspaper in which you explain your point of view on this statement.

[40 Marks]

(AO5 = 24 marks for Content and Organisation; AO6 = 16 marks for Technical Accuracy)

(45/50 Minutes Total = 40 Minutes Writing + 5/10 Minutes Making Notes/Planning/Checking Final Answer for Basic Corrections)

(600 Words Maximum per Essay = 15 Words per Minute)

Does homework need to be abolished?

Homework and its "value", has been the subject of sharp debate among many educational experts and researchers. Some educators argue that homework is beneficial to students as it enhances learning, develops the skills taught in class, and enables educators to verify that students have comprehended their lessons. Proponents also argue that homework makes it more likely that students will develop and maintain effective study habits that they can use throughout their educational career. Homework should also develop time management skills, encourage collaboration between students and engage them in active learning. A study by Bempechat (2004) stated that homework develops students' motivation and that parents and teachers believed that homework improved students' study skills and their sense of personal responsibility.

However, homework has also been identified in numerous studies and articles as a significant source of stress and anxiety for students. Leone & Richards (1989) found that students generally had negative emotions when completing homework and a reduced sense of engagement, compared to other activities. There are gender differences also as U.S. teenage girls spent more time doing homework than U.S. teenage boys. There are also cultural disparities and differences as British students receive more homework than many other countries in Europe, with the weekly average time spent on homework, for an A level subject, being 5 hours. A study of 1,983 students in Hong Kong, also found that homework led not only to increased stress and anxiety, but even to manifested physical symptoms, such as headaches and stomach-aches.

Homework can also cause tension and conflict in the home as well as at school, as some students have reported that teachers and parents frequently criticise their work.

Homework that remains unmarked without feedback from the teacher has little to no effect on the learning of students and a study by the Dresden University of Technology, describes homework as "an educational ritual" that has little to no influence on academic performance. Homework also disrupts a students' extracurricular activities and responsibilities and students who reported stress from homework were also more likely to be deprived of sleep.

Homework is sometimes set in order to punish a student or a class and is sometimes used to outsource school material which was not completed in the classroom to the home. As a consequence, students often have to use the internet or other resources to complete their homework, which provides clear disadvantages for students without internet access. Thus, such homework fails to promote equal opportunities. Also, when educators assign homework, there is often no differentiation applied to the set task by the educator, as each student is usually given the same exercises, regardless of how well the student is performing. This leaves some students with a low degree of challenge while others are overwhelmed. Feeling overwhelmed can also negatively affect a students' natural curiosity and desire for knowledge.

The subject of homework provokes debate. Some students "don't do it at all" and others, (usually from more affluent backgrounds) do "get it done for them;" by their educated parents or private tutors. There is no clear, discernible evidence that homework improves academic performance and it can also create considerable stress for students and parents alike. So, does it have any "value"? Should students solely "...be relaxing in their free time."? I personally believe that only homework with a specific set purpose, that will aid the student in understanding their subject at a deeper level and contribute to the successful undertaking of the examination, (which can lead to the student's academic advancement) is of any lasting or real value to the student.

(600 words)

PAPER 2: SECTION B: WRITING: SECOND ESSAY: NEWSPAPER ARTICLE

You are advised to spend about 45 to 50 minutes on this section.

Write in full sentences.

You are reminded of the need to plan your answer.

You should leave enough time to check your work at the end.

Question: *'Parents today are over-protective. They should let their children take part in adventurous, even risky, activities to prepare them for later life.'*

Write an article for a broadsheet newspaper in which you argue for or against this statement.

[40 Marks]

(AO5 = 24 marks for Content and Organisation; AO6 = 16 marks for Technical Accuracy)

(45/50 Minutes Total = 40 Minutes Writing + 5/10 Minutes Making Notes/Planning/Checking Final Answer for Basic Corrections)

(600 Words Maximum per Essay = 15 Words per Minute)

Do modern, over-protective parents inhibit their child's sense of adventure?

Children go through different stages in life; and as children become adolescents, parents will encounter new challenges as adolescents seek and desire freedom. In later life, these adolescents will soon become adults and the freedom they seek will be theirs, yet, will they be ready for it?

Parents use differing strategies in their child rearing. Parenting styles are the representation of how parents respond to and make demands on their children. There are various theories and opinions on the best ways to rear children.

Authoritarian parents generally tell the child what to do instead of allowing the child to choose by themselves. Children are expected to comply with their parents' rules without question which makes the child appear to excel in the short term but limits development in ways that are increasingly revealed; as negative behaviours continue into adulthood. Indulgent parenting is a style of parenting in which parents are very involved with their children but place few demands or controls on them. Permissive parents also allow children to make their own decisions, giving them advice as a friend. Neglectful parents allow and set no limits on their children. Unlike the indulgent and permissive parents, neglectful parents do this because they are detached from their children's needs.

Authoritative parents set clear standards for their children, monitor the limits that they set, and also allow children to explore more freely and to develop autonomy. They produce children who are more independent and self-reliant. They also expect mature, independent, and age-appropriate behaviour of children. As a result, children of authoritative parents are more likely to be successful, well-liked by those around them, generous and capable of self-determination. Baumrind, a child psychologist, believes that parents should be neither punishing nor apathetic; instead, they should make rules for their children and be affectionate with them. These types of parents often help their children to find appropriate outlets to solve problems and encourage children to be independent yet still place limits on their actions.

Research in parenting and child development has repeatedly found that parents who provide their children with the proper levels of nurture, independence and control, have children who appear to have higher levels of competence and are both self-reliant, and independent. Expressing love and nurturing children with affection also encourages positive physical and mental progress in children.

Frank Furedi is a sociologist who believes that the actions of parents are less decisive than claimed. He describes the term 'infant determinism' as the determination of a person's life prospects by what happens to them during infancy, arguing that there is little or no evidence for its truth. Similarly, the journalist Tim Gill has expressed concern about excessive risk aversion by parents and those responsible for children in his book, 'No Fear.'[1]. This aversion limits the opportunities for children to develop sufficient adult skills, particularly in dealing with risk, but also in performing adventurous activities.

Parents and how they should raise their children, is a contentious issue. Modern day parents may be more protective than their counterparts in previous generations. Adult life is certainly a challenge and childhood ideally prepares children to meet those challenges. In terms of 'risky' activities, I personally would not invite any extra risk into my own, and certainly not into my child's life than the inherent risk that life already provides and that we all must face. As an authoritative parent, adventurous activities are however, I believe, an important part of a child's development and preparation in order to be a responsible, productive and stable adult in 'later life.'

(600 words)

---

[1] Gill, Tim (2007) *No fear: Growing up in a Risk Averse Society*. Calouste Gulbenkian Foundation.

PAPER 2: SECTION B: WRITING: THIRD ESSAY: SPEECH

You are advised to spend about 45 to 50 minutes on this section.

Write in full sentences.

You are reminded of the need to plan your answer.

You should leave enough time to check your work at the end.

Question: *'Education is not just about which school you go to, or what qualifications you gain; it is also about what you learn from your experiences outside of school.'*

Write a speech for your school or college Leavers' Day to explain what you think makes a good education.

[40 Marks]

(AO5 = 24 marks for Content and Organisation; AO6 = 16 marks for Technical Accuracy)

(45/50 Minutes Total = 40 Minutes Writing + 5/10 Minutes Making Notes/Planning/Checking Final Answer for Basic Corrections)

(600 Words Maximum per Essay = 15 Words per Minute)

We have all been taught that having a good education will provide us with comfort, reassurance and peace of mind, not only for ourselves but also for our friends and families. We would all be happier if we felt that we were guaranteed a good education, for who doesn't want success? Yet, what makes a good education?

There are three essential components to a good education: attending the right school, gaining strong qualifications in your chosen area of study and the experiences we have outside of school, with the latter, perhaps, being the most overlooked.

In relation to a good education being heavily linked to which school you attend; this can be exemplified in how the levels of teaching quality differ widely across schools and in how all students do not receive the same level of education nationwide. For example, a female student, in a school in the East Midlands, who wishes to remain anonymous, claims that she was without a regular teacher of Psychology throughout the entirety of her final year before her A level examinations.

In terms of educational qualifications, there are millions of students at the mercy of which subjects can be studied in the curriculum and even with which subjects are being offered in their schools. Many students also do not pick the qualifications that will serve them in their later lives and careers. They spend the duration of their school careers studying school subjects that will have little, if any, relevance at all to their lives after school. Some people might say that students have more choice than ever in terms of what they can study, however, although we have been able to select from a wide range of subjects at our school, there are many schools with a much more limited range of subjects and every school could also be improved upon in this area.

A vast array of studies show that motivation is key to achieving in any area. Yet students too are often uninformed or even uninterested when it comes to receiving the best education possible. And the vast majority of people agree that if students generally received a good quality of education consistently throughout the country that this would subsequently impact all levels of our communities, through decreasing crime to providing an increase in quality services that would change our national community for the better. We can and must respond to the threat of educational inequality throughout this country. If we fail to do so we betray ourselves and subsequent generations.

Experiences outside of school are also a catalyst for increasing our levels of emotional and social intelligence. Extra-curricular activities and sports provide us with the ability to work in a team and to be able to begin to locate where our interests, passions and maximum usefulness to ourselves, our families, friends and society at large, lies.

We, the students, our teachers and the community at large, are the key to good quality education and it is of primary importance also that we manage our time outside of school in order to educate ourselves and to maximise our potential; as this will impact our lives radically going forward.

We each have massive potential and capability and when we, both students and teachers, attempt to fully engage with our innermost qualities, we create a pathway to a good quality education for all. This can be provided through good quality teaching, in a fitting and well purposed academic environment that offers a wide range of educational subjects; tailored to meet students' needs. Ultimately, this is how we provide a good education for all.

(600 words)

PAPER 2: SECTION B: WRITING: FOURTH ESSAY: NEWSPAPER ARTICLE

You are advised to spend about 45 to 50 minutes on this section.

Write in full sentences.

You are reminded of the need to plan your answer.

You should leave enough time to check your work at the end.

Question: *'All sport should be fun, fair and open to everyone. These days, sport seems to be more about money, corruption and winning at any cost.'*

Write an article for a newspaper in which you explain your point of view on this statement.

[40 Marks]

(AO5 = 24 marks for Content and Organisation; AO6 = 16 marks for Technical Accuracy)

(45/50 Minutes Total = 40 Minutes Writing + 5/10 Minutes Making Notes/Planning/Checking Final Answer for Basic Corrections)

(600 Words Maximum per Essay = 15 Words per Minute)

The high stakes of sport: Corruption, inaccessibility and the phenomenon of sportswashing.

For those young people who are on the cusp of a professional and highly lucrative sports career, can their conditioned, aggressively competitive attitude and their desire for the financial rewards professional sport can accrue, affect their mental well-being? Psychological studies found that 55% of players suffered mentally from depression, anxiety and 'Post Traumatic Stress Disorder' (PTSD) 21 days after being released from football academies. This appears to exemplify a winning at all costs attitude in professional sport; and to the significant detriment of those attempting to participate in it.

Corruption has, at times, been synonymous with professional sport. Over 23 boxers and 7 promoters were revealed to have been involved in fights that involved bribery. Football has had match fixing scandals and the Colombian football player Andres Escobar, was executed by a drug cartel, after his own goal eliminated Colombia from the 1994 World Cup. More recently, there have been gambling controversies whereby an independent regulatory commission found that Ivan Toney repeatedly placed bets on matches in which his own team were involved. The Russian figure skater Kamila Valieva also recently tested positive for a heart medication that is banned in sports. In addition to the corruption found within professional sport, it also remains inaccessible to all people, as many are frequently precluded by a lack of financial means to participate in sport and to even watch it live on television. Live sport such as Champions league football games are shown exclusively on subscription channels and elite boxing events are pay per view. This is financially prohibitive for many people.

The phenomenon of sportswashing refers to the use of an athletic event to promote an individual, corporation or a government, especially amid controversy or scandal. A recent example of sportswashing is believed to be Qatar's hosting of the 2022 FIFA World Cup. However, it is not simply a recent phenomenon. Perhaps the most notorious example of sportswashing is the 1936 Olympic Games in Berlin, which has been termed the 'Nazi Olympics.'. At the time, there were unsuccessful calls for a boycott against the racist regime of Adolf Hitler, which in turn, assured the International Olympic Committee that qualified Jewish athletes would participate, yet barred or prevented Jewish athletes from taking part, through a variety of discriminatory and highly unfair methods.

The Saudi Arabia crown prince Mohammed bin Salman recently stated that he does not care about accusations of 'sportswashing', if it continues to increase Saudi Arabia's 'Gross Domestic Product' (GDP). Saudi Arabia's Public Investment Fund (PIF) led the takeover of Newcastle United last year and launched LIV Golf and is lavishing money on soccer, Formula 1 racing, cricket and boxing also. Last year, Newcastle United revealed a kit which clearly resembled the Saudi Arabia national team kit and Amnesty International stated that this was a clear example of sportswashing. Meanwhile, Saudi Arabia has been heavily criticised for its human rights violations, through mass executions, women's rights abuses, the criminalisation of homosexuality, the restriction of free speech and the war in Yemen.

In conclusion, I personally believe that highly profitable, elite professional sport is overly commercialised and that it is now mainly a symbol of greed, profit and even corruption at times; with a clearly resounding message of winning at any cost. While all sport should display the imperative qualities of being fair and fun with accessible opportunities for all, sadly I believe that this is increasingly becoming a fantasy as capitalism, corruption and greed become prevailing dark forces that are both shaping and tainting the modern-day sports industry.

(600 words)

PAPER 2: SECTION B: WRITING: FIFTH ESSAY: LETTER

You are advised to spend about 45 to 50 minutes on this section.

Write in full sentences.

You are reminded of the need to plan your answer.

You should leave enough time to check your work at the end.

Question: *'Cars are noisy, dirty, smelly and downright dangerous. They should be banned from all town and city centres, allowing people to walk and cycle in peace.'*

Write a letter to the Minister for Transport arguing your point of view on this statement.

[40 Marks]

(AO5 = 24 marks for Content and Organisation; AO6 = 16 marks for Technical Accuracy)

(45/50 Minutes Total = 40 Minutes Writing + 5/10 Minutes Making Notes/Planning/Checking Final Answer for Basic Corrections)

(600 Words Maximum per Essay = 15 Words per Minute)

(In the letter examples in this book, I will provide a date minus the sender and recipients' address.)

15th September 2023

Dear Minister for Transport,

I am writing in response to a statement as regards whether '...cars should be banned from all town and city centres,' thus '...allowing people to walk and cycle in peace.'. As the Minister for Transport, I believe that you are the most suitable individual for me to contact as regards this issue. This letter hopefully enables me to expand upon the points presented in the statement and to elucidate my own views on this topic.

As a child, I often mused as to why half the earth was asphalt, (as it seemed to appear to me) as I played outside. Once, in my younger days, I also visited Rottnest Island, an island off the coast of Western Australia. Private cars to this day are not allowed on the island and the most common transport is by bicycle or walking. Tropical fish, dolphins and sea lions flourished in crystal clear, turquoise waters unaffected by the pollution of ever-present cars. It was a once in a lifetime experience!

The statement initially declares that 'Cars are noisy, dirty, smelly and downright dangerous.'. I would temper this somewhat and instead concede that cars can emit high levels of noise, have varying levels of dirt upon their carriage, have a distinctive smell and can at times be dangerous, however, these factors are to a large extent, dependent on the owners of the vehicles also. To further ameliorate the issues that cars present in our modern world, there has been the advent of the electric car, self-driving cars and the widespread creation of cycle lanes throughout the country. Car-pooling and train travel have also been heavily promoted (although the latter has been heavily affected by persistent train strikes).

The most serious issue and a particularly pressing concern that I believe must be addressed from the statement is whether, 'Cars are ...downright dangerous.'. Statistics state that road traffic crashes now represent the eighth leading cause of death throughout the world. There are more than 1.35 million lives lost each year in automobile accidents and they cause up to 50 million injuries per year. The road safety agency 'Brake' states that in the United Kingdom alone, in 2021, 1608 people were killed and 26701 people were seriously injured in car accidents. This illustrates the graveness of our current situation.

There are also further problems resulting from the cars that we drive and the oil that we use, due to the production and burning of fossil fuels. This has a harmful effect on all of us, particularly those of us in large cities and the toxic emissions generated propel climate change. In contrast, during the Covid lockdowns, there was evidence that the reduction in passenger transport demand caused a temporary reduction in global greenhouse gas emissions and air pollution.

In conclusion, and after taking some time to consider how any law changes you may implement will affect hard-working families, I do concede that cars are necessary at the present time for practical purposes. This is particularly evident in terms of cost-effectiveness for families travelling with young children and in cities with poor public transport infrastructure and options which provide no feasible alternatives or public hire cycle schemes. However, I also believe that it is important to understand that one of the biggest negative and detrimental impacts on our modern way of life is the cars that are on our already overcrowded roads and I personally believe that there should be no cars in our '...town and city centres' thus '...allowing people to walk and cycle in peace.'.

Yours sincerely,

Joseph Anthony Campbell

(600 words)

PAPER 2: SECTION B: WRITING: SIXTH ESSAY: LETTER

You are advised to spend about 45 to 50 minutes on this section.

Write in full sentences.

You are reminded of the need to plan your answer.

You should leave enough time to check your work at the end.

Question: *'It is people who have extraordinary skill, courage and determination who deserve to be famous, not those who have good looks or lots of money or behave badly.'*

Write a letter to the editor of a newspaper in which you argue your point of view in response to this statement.

[40 Marks]

(AO5 = 24 marks for Content and Organisation; AO6 = 16 marks for Technical Accuracy)

(45/50 Minutes Total = 40 Minutes Writing + 5/10 Minutes Making Notes/Planning/Checking Final Answer for Basic Corrections)

(600 Words Maximum per Essay = 15 Words per Minute)

(In the letter examples in this book, I will provide a date minus the sender and recipients' address.)

13th May 2023

Dear Mr Giles-White,

I am writing in response to your statement as regards who deserves to be famous. As the editor of the newspaper, I believe that you are the most suitable individual for me to contact. This letter hopefully enables me to expand upon your statement and on my own views as regards this topic.

I believe that it is important to ask: Does anyone deserve to be famous? Does it provide the person themselves with anything inherently valuable? An early 19th century female French writer, Madame de Stael, stated that, "Fame is the shining bereavement of happiness."[2]. Perspective may be one of the first casualties of fame. Losing perspective means not seeing things as they are in actuality. Perhaps we need to puncture the myth of celebrity and of the distorting lens that is fame, as it is confounding to elevate those, as mentioned in your statement, that '...have good looks or lots of money or behave badly.'.

Celebrity may be an illusory term foisted by others upon certain individuals, yet it can create a platform in the world, which can be used for noble purposes. Paul Hewson, known as Bono, for example, has used his celebrity for noble and admirable purposes. He has been instrumental in ensuring debt cancellation for Africa's poorest countries and in providing affordable treatment for millions of people with HIV (Human Immunodeficiency Virus) in Africa. Nelson Mandela used his fame to end apartheid in his home country and to lead it nobly as its President. Albert Einstein, also never identified with the collective view of his fame and remained humble throughout his

---

[2] *Bono on Bono: Conversations with Michka Assayas* (2005)

life. In these people we recognise the reverence of lives lived with integrity. All people respond to those individuals who live by their principles and bravely face the injustice, prejudice and devastation of the world.

For some people, the magnetism of fame and celebrity are magical. Although it is an illusion, people attempt to get access to celebrities in the hope that some of their good fortune will attach itself to them. A famous person's real identity becomes obscured by a collective view of that person. There is an overvaluation of fame in our modern world, which some famous people begin to identify with and then they begin to see themselves as superior to ordinary people. This results in them becoming more alienated, more unhappy and more dependent on their fame and incapable of genuine, loving relationships. Fame can also make the people with it feel particularly uncomfortable in public and there can be an ambivalence to celebrity; even from the celebrities themselves! Some famous people become desperately unhappy and reclusive as it cannot cure the deep-rooted internal issues a person may have. And some individuals '...behave badly' and even commit crimes in their search for fame; which is insane!

In conclusion, fame can provide a platform to combat the injustices of the world and to help those in need and the purpose of using love and compassion to serve others truly moves people. Yet, asides from this, and in response to the statement, I personally cannot help but wonder if fame would be a blessing or a curse to any person who possessed it. It is clear that people such as nurses, teachers, doctors or firemen are some of the people with '...extraordinary skill, courage and determination', as mentioned in the statement. Contrastingly, celebrities have been incredibly fortunate to be recognised for their talents, yet as to whether they are somehow more important than others, I believe this is simply not true.

Yours sincerely,

Joseph Anthony Campbell

(600 words)

PAPER 2: SECTION B: WRITING: SEVENTH ESSAY: NEWS WEBSITE: ARTICLE

You are advised to spend about 45 to 50 minutes on this section.

Write in full sentences.

You are reminded of the need to plan your answer.

You should leave enough time to check your work at the end.

Question: *'People have become obsessed with travelling ever further and faster. However, travel is expensive, dangerous, damaging and a foolish waste of time!'*

Write an article for a news website in which you argue your point of view on this statement.

[40 Marks]

(AO5 = 24 marks for Content and Organisation; AO6 = 16 marks for Technical Accuracy)

(45/50 Minutes Total = 40 Minutes Writing + 5/10 Minutes Making Notes/Planning/Checking Final Answer for Basic Corrections)

(600 Words Maximum per Essay = 15 Words per Minute)

The road less travelled?

The increased expansion of travel can be traced back to colonialism, when developed countries travelled to and exploited underdeveloped nations during colonial times. However, for thousands of years, the human race has been travelling further and faster and obsessing over how to make the process more efficient. Yet, as transportation prices increase, have we now reached a stage whereby travel is increasingly becoming an expensive, impractical and foolish waste of time?

In the last century, people have frequently attempted travelling ever further and faster. Charles Lindbergh was an American aviator who rose to international fame in 1927, after becoming the first person to fly solo across the Atlantic Ocean. In 1935, Amelia Earhart became the first person to fly solo across both the Atlantic and Pacific Oceans. However, travelling can also be both dangerous and damaging, as two years later, during an attempt to fly around the world, Amelia Earhart was declared missing and presumed dead. There have also been the Apollo shuttle disasters. During a pre-flight test on Apollo 1 on January 27th, 1967, on what was to be the first crewed Apollo mission, a fire cost the lives of three U.S. astronauts. Additionally, on January 28th, 1986, the Space Shuttle 'Challenger', tragically disintegrated 73 seconds into its flight; killing all seven crew members on board.

Perhaps the most famous travelling feat was Apollo 11, the American spaceflight that first landed humans on the Moon. Neil Armstrong and Buzz Aldrin successfully landed the 'Apollo Lunar Module Eagle' on July 20th, 1969. However, financial inequalities frustrated many citizens then, who wondered why the money spent on the Apollo space program was not instead being better spent by taking care of humans on Earth. By 1973, 59% of people believed that spending on space exploration should be reduced.

In our current times, Elon Musk's 'SpaceX Mars' program hopes to facilitate the colonisation of Mars. It is claimed that this is necessary for the long-term survival of the human species and that this will ultimately reduce space transportation costs. However, the program has been criticised as being financially impractical and many doubt whether human life can ever be sustained on Mars.

Meanwhile, back here on Earth, travelling impacts the environment. Travelling is not an eco-friendly activity. As networks of transportation expand and increase, this correlates with an increasing negative impact on our environment. Vehicles continue to cause global warming through carbon dioxide emissions, with these greenhouse gases contributing significantly to global warming. Train travel has also been heavily promoted, yet persistent train strikes have recently been combined with increasing transportation costs.

To conclude, travelling is expensive, time-consuming and it harms the environment. It can also be considered impractical and financially profligate, such as in building rockets to Mars. It is also clear that travelling can be dangerous and damaging, with vehicle accidents being a leading cause of death. On a more mundane level, I also believe that waiting for transportation and taking transportation is frequently frustrating at times. I also do not believe that the quality of transport has improved at a rate which justifies the highly expensive costs of travel. However, I also do not believe that travelling is a total waste of money or a waste of time, if you reach the destination, you truly desire. At times, people travelling further and faster has also provoked in me a sense of awe and wonder, such as when Neil Armstrong took his first steps on the Moon. I, therefore, believe that travelling has been and will continue to be, a vitally important aspect of the human experience.

(600 words)

PAPER 2: SECTION B: WRITING: EIGHTH ESSAY: MAGAZINE ARTICLE

You are advised to spend about 45 to 50 minutes on this section.

Write in full sentences.

You are reminded of the need to plan your answer.

You should leave enough time to check your work at the end.

Question: *'People protest about the cruelty of keeping animals in captivity, but they seem happy enough to eat meat, keep pets and visit zoos. All animals should be free!'*

Write an article for a magazine in which you explain your point of view on this statement.

[40 Marks]

(AO5 = 24 marks for Content and Organisation; AO6 = 16 marks for Technical Accuracy)

(45/50 Minutes Total = 40 Minutes Writing + 5/10 Minutes Making Notes/Planning/Checking Final Answer for Basic Corrections)

(600 Words Maximum per Essay = 15 Words per Minute)

Are we ready for animal emancipation?

The relationship between human beings and animals could be interpreted as contradictory. People 'eat meat' yet 'keep pets' and 'protest about... cruelty' yet 'visit zoos.'. The consumption of meat and animal products alongside the practice of animal testing from the potentially exploitative cosmetic and pharmaceutical industries, is prevalent throughout our culture. It is vitally important, therefore, that we aim to decipher these contradictions as we establish our views on how animals should be treated.

In our society, there are people who eat meat and there are vegetarians who do not eat meat and flexitarians who have primarily vegetarian diets but occasionally eat meat or fish. Veganism, which appears to be a growing trend in mainstream society, involves abstaining from the use of animal products in one's diet and rejects the status of animals as mere commodities.

Animal exploitation is often linked with animal testing, which is the use of non-human animals in experiments. 'The Royal Society for the Prevention of Cruelty to Animals' (RSPCA) states that in the United Kingdom alone, approximately 3.06 million scientific procedures, involving four million living animals, were carried out in 2021. While testing on animals in the United Kingdom is legal, it is only allowed if the benefits gained from the research outweigh any animal suffering. This argument is frequently proffered when testing medicines. However, animal testing experiments are also used for household cleaning products, agricultural chemicals and food additives.

Perhaps the most contradictory relationship humans have with animals is in peoples' protestations as regards 'keeping animals in captivity' and yet the fact that many people 'visit zoos'. There are accredited zoos, which are part of 'The Association of Zoos and Aquariums'. There is also a clear argument that zoos can help to save endangered species through providing them with a relatively safe environment; protected from poachers and predators. Breeding programmes are another way to protect endangered species. Zoos also have an educational aspect as people learn about animals by viewing them in person. This can also engender empathy within people for a species that is facing extinction in the wild. However, animals in captivity can frequently suffer and captivity is an artificial alternative to being free in the wild. As a dolphin performs routine tricks at 'Sea World', is this an equitable contrast to a dolphin emerging natural and free from the surface of the ocean? Is it ever possible for all of the needs of these animals to be met in an environment separated from the natural world?

This apparent contradiction in relation to our behaviour with animals is again shown in how people who keep cats, dogs and other pets also '...protest about the cruelty of keeping animals in captivity'. However, some animals are domesticated and they are genetically distinct from their wild ancestors. Dogs were most likely domesticated from grey wolves and dogs' scientific name is 'canis lupus familiaris,' while the grey wolves name is 'canis lupus'. Domesticated animals live alongside humans. There are hundreds of domestic dog species today.

To conclude, as regards the statement of whether 'All animals should be free!', I personally believe that certain animals require human care due to their levels of domestication. Many humans also need the companionship and love of animals. However, I also believe that animals should be emancipated from zoos, should not be tested upon and that they should not be used as food. However, humans' relationship with animals is contradictory and until we address these contradictions, I believe that we will be unable to progress in the provision of a widespread emancipation of captive animals.

(600 words)

PAPER 2: SECTION B: WRITING: NINTH ESSAY: LETTER

You are advised to spend about 45 to 50 minutes on this section.

Write in full sentences.

You are reminded of the need to plan your answer.

You should leave enough time to check your work at the end.

Question: *'Festivals and fairs should be banned. They encourage bad behaviour and are disruptive to local communities.'*

Write a letter to your local newspaper in which you argue for or against this statement.

[40 Marks]

(AO5 = 24 marks for Content and Organisation; AO6 = 16 marks for Technical Accuracy)

(45/50 Minutes Total = 40 Minutes Writing + 5/10 Minutes Making Notes/Planning/Checking Final Answer for Basic Corrections)

(600 Words Maximum per Essay = 15 Words per Minute)

(In the letter examples in this book, I will provide a date minus the sender and recipients' address.)

22nd September 2023

Dear Sir or Madam,

I am writing in response to the statement made in your newspaper which stated that all: 'Festivals and fairs should be banned.'. This letter hopefully enables me to examine the points presented in the statement and to clarify my own views on this topic.

A further point in the statement is that festivals and fairs '...encourage bad behaviour'. I am fully aware that such fairs and festivals can involve the use of alcohol and drugs and that vandalism has been reported within the vicinity of the area of festivals. Excessive litter at festivals can have a negative impact on the environment and overcrowding also exacerbates the risk of injuries. There are also those who have unfortunately been the victims of theft and criminality during events.

The statement further remonstrates that festivals and fairs are '...disruptive to local communities.'. The excessive noise emitted can be a heavy disturbance to some neighbourhoods within close proximity. Neighbouring communities may also feel that they tarnish the local community's image and reputation. There is also a debate as to whether the workers at festivals and fairs are exploited or contrastingly whether they are provided with much needed and valued work?

However, there are also many positives that can be gleaned from festivals and fairs. Even Elvis Presley himself began his legendary career as the main feature of 'Cotton Carnival' opening night almost 70 years ago. Festivals and fairs are a way for people to forge new friendships and to create lasting memories. People of similar interests are able to make connections and are led to new ways of thinking. There is freedom, self-expression, connections, relationships and bonds forged. Festivals and fairs remain both a vibrant and vital part of our society and culture; unifying communities and diverse people of differing backgrounds.

There is also a clear economic boost for communities, through local businesses being able to benefit from festivals and fairs through the associated tourism and the influx of visitors they provide. This helps small businesses, restaurants and local retailers to experience and prosper from an increase in economic traction through the increased footfall that is provided by festivals and fairs. Furthermore, the economic stability and well-being this provides to local communities could be argued to be more important than the potential disruption and predominantly low levels of anti-social behaviour that festivals and fairs can cause.

For those who love festivals and fairs and for those who wish to ban them, it is hard when facing these diametrically opposed views, to comprehend one another. The advantages and disadvantages of festivals and fairs illuminates the fact that there are many elements to consider. For some, festivals and fairs bring so much joy, connection and economic prosperity that it is unthinkable to eliminate them. However, as previously mentioned, they can be 'disruptive' and '…encourage bad behaviour'.

In conclusion, I completely comprehend and empathise with the concerns of those who experience disruption and anti-social behaviour during festivals and fairs. I personally believe that it is vital that we aim to remove and reduce, as much as possible, these aforementioned negative aspects of festivals and fairs without banning them entirely; as they are a vital part of many people's lives. Fortunately, it only appears to be a minority of people that attend festivals and fairs that create a disturbance. However, reducing and ultimately aiming to fix community tensions as regards festivals and fairs is vitally important in maintaining local well-being and for preserving the long-term viability of these events. Thank you for taking these ideas into consideration.

Yours faithfully,

Joseph Anthony Campbell

(600 words)

PAPER 2: SECTION B: WRITING: TENTH ESSAY: SPEECH

You are advised to spend about 45 to 50 minutes on this section.

Write in full sentences.

You are reminded of the need to plan your answer.

You should leave enough time to check your work at the end.

Question: *'Floods, earthquakes, hurricanes and landslides – we see more and more reports of environmental disasters affecting the world and its people every day.'*

Write the text of a speech for a debate at your school or college in which you persuade young people to take more responsibility for protecting the environment.

[40 Marks]

(AO5 = 24 marks for Content and Organisation; AO6 = 16 marks for Technical Accuracy)

(45/50 Minutes Total = 40 Minutes Writing + 5/10 Minutes Making Notes/Planning/Checking Final Answer for Basic Corrections)

(600 Words Maximum per Essay = 15 Words per Minute)

In 2019, the United Kingdom became the first national government to declare a climate emergency and today, a majority of people, view it as a global emergency. Students, like ourselves, are taking part in global demonstrations such as the 'School Strike for Climate' which was inspired by Greta Thunberg and are making sure their voices are heard.

The effects of climate change on humans have been observed worldwide and can now be observed on all continents and ocean regions. We may all know the negative ramifications of climate change upon our environment but I believe they need to be made clear, in order to understand the level of the task that we are facing!

The 'World Health Organisation' has stated that climate change is our greatest threat to global health in the 21st century. Extreme weather already leads to loss of life and a variety of infectious diseases are transmitted more easily in a warmer climate. Extreme weather also leads to crop failures and both children and older people are the most vulnerable to extreme heat. Through higher levels of Carbon Dioxide in the atmosphere, the size and speed of global warming will result in the extinction of many species. Melting ice from polar ice caps is leading to an increase in the flow of freshwater into the world's oceans and an increase in the level of rainfall means that flooding is more common. There is a rapid intensification of hurricanes and major geological hazards such as earthquakes, which result in landslides, throughout the world. Global warming therefore, has potentially irreversible consequences for both people and ecosystems. The 'World Health Organisation' has also estimated that over 500,000 more deaths are projected yearly until 2050 due to the subsequent reduction in both food availability and quality. However, countries that are most vulnerable to climate change are only responsible for a small percentage of the global emissions of Carbon Dioxide. This is both unjust and unfair and the 'World Bank' estimates that climate change could plummet over 100 million people into poverty by 2030. In 7 years', time!

As we can clearly observe, protecting the environment is a 'now' problem, rather than a 'future' problem. It is the responsibility of our generation and of all the generations on the planet at this time, to protect our home; our planet. But how can we do this?

In our lifetime, we will need to move towards using electricity generated from low-carbon sources. Our first car could be an electric one, which helps drive towards the change needed. And if we cannot afford this yet, we always have the option of public transport or more active modes of transport such as cycling and walking, which also keeps us fit and healthy!

The production of meat and dairy is also responsible for approximately three quarters of all emissions from agriculture. We could therefore reduce or even eliminate meat from our diets and help to protect our planet. Our houses could also use solar panels and this benefits the environment as renewable energy is key to limiting the negative impact of climate change on the environment. We can all take measures to conserve energy through using only the energy we need as efficient energy conservation reduces our carbon footprint and this aids a global transition to clean energy development.

We all have the potential to be a part of the solution. We are all a part of the world. Through taking responsibility for our environment, we are taking responsibility for ourselves and the future generations to come.

Thank you for allowing me to talk with you today.

(600 words)

PAPER 2: SECTION B: WRITING: ELEVENTH ESSAY: NEWSPAPER ARTICLE

You are advised to spend about 45 to 50 minutes on this section.

Write in full sentences.

You are reminded of the need to plan your answer.

You should leave enough time to check your work at the end.

Question: *'Libraries are now simply buildings from the past. The world has now moved online. Library buildings should be knocked down and put to better use.'*

Write an article for a broadsheet newspaper in which you explain your point of view on this statement.

[40 Marks]

(AO5 = 24 marks for Content and Organisation; AO6 = 16 marks for Technical Accuracy)

(45/50 Minutes Total = 40 Minutes Writing + 5/10 Minutes Making Notes/Planning/Checking Final Answer for Basic Corrections)

(600 Words Maximum per Essay = 15 Words per Minute)

Can libraries survive in the digital age?

A library is a collection of materials, books and media that are easily accessible to the general public. For some, the beauty of the library is that it is a sanctuary; a place that provides peaceful focus and learning. Libraries, however, provide both quiet and conducive areas for studying, as well as areas for group study and collaboration. Physical books, which are provided by the library, may also be considered more reliable than website material for students who use reference material as they have been through a rigorous process of fact finding and editing that is harder to achieve with online resources. Although some patrons may not know how to fully use the library's resources, a key benefit of libraries are the services of librarians, who are trained experts at finding, selecting, organising and interpreting peoples' information needs. Libraries are also community hubs, where programs are delivered and people can engage in lifelong learning.

The emergence of the internet, and the digital age, however, leads some to believe that the resulting decline in library usage, puts the necessity of these services in considerable doubt. In the 21st century, there has been an ever-increasing use of the internet to both gather and retrieve data. Retrieving information from the internet is also considered to be more efficient and less time consuming than visiting a traditional library. This shift to 'digital libraries' has greatly impacted the way people use physical libraries. Therefore, it is true that libraries need to address the ways that they market their services, in order to compete in the digital age and thus ameliorate the risk of losing its users. However, the marketing of its services has to be financially supported in order for it to be successful. This could be problematic for publicly funded library services.

As the prominence of and our reliance on the internet has grown, libraries are now becoming a part of the digital world. In addition to providing print resources, libraries also provide public facilities for access to their electronic resources as they move their emphasis from providing print resources to providing more computers and more internet access. There is also an increased availability of e-resources in libraries and the digitisation of books, particularly those that are out-of-print, provides resources for library and other online users. Libraries now provide both physical, hard copy documents or digital access materials (known as soft copies), and libraries may even be based in a physical location or even a virtual space; or provide both facilities. There is also the adoption of electronic catalogue databases and all content is now held on bibliographic databases. This transition towards the digitisation of libraries is exemplified for example, in the 'Bibliotheca Alexandrina' in Alexandria, Egypt, where there are both physical stacks and computer terminals side by side.

To conclude, I believe that libraries are valuable resources. Although libraries in their past physical form would be considered antiquated in our digital age, as the world has moved online, I believe that libraries are rising to meet those challenges as they move with the digital age. Although progress has been gradual, it appears that there is now a synergy developing. Libraries are also important community hubs and serve a larger purpose than simply providing physical and digital resources as they are a place where people can learn to use the internet through staff members support and assistance, and where people can take classes and be a part of community outreach services. They should therefore remain standing and continue to provide both information and extremely important community services.

(600 words)

PAPER 2: SECTION B: WRITING: TWELFTH ESSAY: NEWSPAPER ARTICLE

You are advised to spend about 45 to 50 minutes on this section.

Write in full sentences.

You are reminded of the need to plan your answer.

You should leave enough time to check your work at the end.

Question: *'Social media is responsible for many of the stresses of modern life for young people. Young people would have a better quality of life without social media.'*

Write an article for a broadsheet newspaper in which you explain your point of view on this statement.

[40 Marks]

(AO5 = 24 marks for Content and Organisation; AO6 = 16 marks for Technical Accuracy)

(45/50 Minutes Total = 40 Minutes Writing + 5/10 Minutes Making Notes/Planning/Checking Final Answer for Basic Corrections)

(600 Words Maximum per Essay = 15 Words per Minute)

Would young people have a better quality of life without social media?

Social media and social networking are prevalent among both younger and older generations, to the extent of undermining the formerly authoritative voices of traditional news media. Amongst young people, social media use has vastly increased since the COVID pandemic. There have been clear benefits to social media through being able to be connected to one another during nationwide lockdowns. However, the negative effects of social media have been compounded during this time also.

One phenomenon within social media is the issue of social comparison. Young people are motivated to portray themselves in a positive light and as young people compare their own lives to the lives of their friends through their posts, this can have severely negative effects on both their physical and mental health. Social media images also allow for people to be inundated with 'celebrity' and influencer 'images' which can lead to negative self-comparison. A study by King university stated that 87% of women and 65% of men compared themselves to images presented on social media. However, there have been efforts to combat these negative effects, such as #instagramversusreality, in an effort to promote body positivity.

There are clear emotional effects to the use of social media by young people. According to a study from the University of Pittsburgh, there is a strong relationship between the use of social media and experiencing sleep disturbance; which has significant ramifications for young adults' health and well-being. Depression has also been found to affect adolescents who engage extensively with social media sites. This can also result in reclusiveness and create feelings of isolation and low self-esteem among young people. Self-esteem is also positively affected by positive comments on social media and negatively affected by negative comments. This affects young people's sense of self-worth.

Young people who self-diagnose addiction-like symptoms in their social media usage are also more likely to report low self-esteem and depressive symptoms through experiencing feelings of ambivalence, emotional exhaustion, and depersonalisation. There are also many negative interpersonal interactions between users through cyberbullying, online harassment, and 'trolling'; with over 50% of young people reporting that they have been bullied online! The various negative emotional effects that can be experienced in a young person's use of social media can negatively impact their psychological health and well-being and in extreme, tragic cases, it has even been linked to incidents of suicide.

Contrastingly, social media can have a supportive effect on the individuals who use it. Many people have found their future spouse through social media sites. Social justice issues and support groups can be maintained or even created through social media sites. It can also facilitate positive discussion for professionals and students alike, and provide a supportive community for individuals who differ from the mainstream. This can create a sense of community whereby people provide support to one another through positive tweets, likes, and comments.

Although there are clearly positive attributes to the use of social media for young people and older people alike, I believe personally that social media usage is a significant contributor to the stresses of modern life and can be particularly detrimental to the mental health of young people. I believe that young people would have a better quality of life overall without social media yet I am fully aware that social media is a phenomenon that is here to stay. I believe that social media companies should work together to ameliorate its evidently negative effects and that the primary focus of social media should be to protect all of its users; particularly young people.

(600 words)

TOP TIPS FOR A GRADE 9 WHEN WRITING ARTICLES, SPEECHES AND LETTERS

ARTICLES

The articles that you have to create from your question paper may be a newspaper article for a broadsheet, (referred to as the quality press), or a tabloid newspaper, (referred to as the popular press). You may also have to write a magazine article or an article for a news website. A broadsheet newspaper article has a headline, uses more formal language and takes a more serious tone than a non-broadsheet newspaper article, or a magazine or news website article; whereby your readers may be a broader group of people.

An article is a piece of writing about a particular topic. Although an article may offer a balanced view of the set statement from your question, at some point in your article, you will have to present your own opinion.

Fundamentally, a newspaper article has a bold headline and is divided into paragraphs. The basic structure of an article for a newspaper, magazine or website, is usually in three parts: The opening, introductory paragraph should aim to engage the reader and outline the principal points of the article.

The middle paragraphs in the article are a series of paragraphs that provide more detail and may counterbalance the positive and negative aspects of the given statement or may follow one clear line of argument throughout.

A concluding paragraph (and the latest point whereby you can give your viewpoint on the given statement) draws the main points together and may provide the reader with a circular structure, in which the conclusion connects back to your opening paragraph. Frequently, in an article, writers also tend to lead to their most important point.

SPEECHES

The purpose of the speech that you will create from your question paper is to impress upon your listeners, a particular point of view. The language used is therefore of a typically persuasive nature. However, you may also be asked to give your viewpoint on a certain topic. The language you use in a speech will also vary depending on your audience. In a speech to a professional audience, formal language is the most appropriate.

Your speech should follow a three-part structure:

The opening, introductory paragraph should aim to be highly engaging, inspirational and/or motivational.

The middle paragraphs should include a well-structured argument, with several main points that include countering objections which may be raised to your argument.

A concluding paragraph draws the main points together and may provide the listener with a circular structure, in which the conclusion connects back to your opening paragraph. This should then aim to lead to both dynamic and memorable concluding lines.

Ten persuasive language devices for your speech.

Here are 10 persuasive, linguistic devices that you could include in your speech, to make it more dynamic and memorable:

1. Rhetorical question. This is asked to make a point or for effect, rather than to elicit an answer.
2. Rule of threes (Triples). Grouping the language that you use, (through words or ideas), into 'threes', makes it more memorable and persuasive.

3. Emotive language. This is language that appeals to the emotions.
4. Handling objections. This is when you counter objections that may be raised to your argument.
5. Hyperbole. This is using exaggerated language for effect.
6. Anecdote. This is using real life examples that support your argument.
7. Statistics and figures. It helps to use factual data when it is used in a persuasive argument.
8. Personal pronouns. Using 'we', 'I' and 'you' makes your audience feel more included.
9. Flattery. Complimenting your audience can help you to be more persuasive.
10. Imperatives. Forceful, instructional language can also bolster your argument.

Ultimately, when writing a speech, you should aim to shape the language you use to match your audience and your purpose, through addressing the audience directly, and including persuasive language and a rousing tone; particularly in the last paragraph.

LETTERS

The purpose of the letter that you will create from your question paper is to impress upon your recipient, a particular point of view.

In a formal letter, the convention is to use Standard English. Formal language is also used. The tone of your letter will vary depending on your purpose and the person that you are asked to write a letter to, for example; this could be, a local newspaper, an editor or a political figure. The level of formality in your language should be matched to the recipient that you are writing your letter to.

Similar to the article, your letter is a piece of writing about a particular topic. Although your letter may offer a balanced view of the given statement from your question, at some point in your letter, you will have to present your own opinion.

Your reader might be one particular person, as with an email or letter.

A formal letter has a conventional structure. The sender's postal address is placed in the top right-hand corner and the recipient's postal address is written to the left and slightly below this, with the date underneath. A letter then opens with the greeting 'Dear...'. If you do not know the name of the person you are writing to, the accepted convention of letter writing is to start your letter with: 'Dear Sir/Madam'.

Again, the basic structure of your letter is in three parts.
The opening, introductory paragraph should aim to engage the reader and outline the principal points of the purpose of your letter.

The middle paragraphs should provide more detail and may counterbalance the positive and negative aspects of the given statement or may follow one line of argument throughout.

A concluding paragraph (and the latest point whereby you can give your viewpoint on the given statement) draws the main points together and may provide the reader with a circular structure, in which the conclusion again connects back to your opening points. The initial paragraph usually outlines the overall aim of the letter, and the conclusion summarises the main points.

Conventionally, there are two different ways to end a letter, depending on the addressee.

If you have named the recipient at the start of your letter, it ends with, 'Yours sincerely'.

If you have not named the recipient at the start of your letter, it ends with, 'Yours faithfully'.

ASSESSMENT OBJECTIVES

The Assessment Objectives are not provided in the examination itself. However, I have provided which assessment objectives are being assessed in the practice questions in this book. It is important to be aware of the structure of how the assessment objectives are allocated in each question of the examination, in order to maximise your opportunities to obtain full marks in each question.

It is often a good idea also to briefly plan your answer before you begin writing it. A plan will mean you answer the question in an organised and sequenced manner. Your newfound understanding of the assessment objectives will also ensure you have met all of the required criteria.

There are **two assessment objectives** assessed in the English Language Paper 2 Section B examination: (**AO5 = 24 marks for Content and Organisation; AO6 = 16 marks for Technical Accuracy**).

<u>AO5 = Content and Organisation (24 marks)</u>

For a Grade 9:

Content: Communicate clearly, effectively and imaginatively. Select and adapt tone, style and register for different forms, purposes and audiences. Your communication must be convincing and compelling with an extensive and ambitious use of vocabulary and a sustained crafting of linguistic devices.

Organisation: Organise information and ideas, using structural and grammatical features to support coherence. Organisation will be provided through a varied and inventive use of structural features. Your writing must be compelling, incorporating a range of convincing and complex ideas and fluently link paragraphs with seamlessly integrated discourse.

AO6 = Technical Accuracy (16 marks)

For a Grade 9:

Technical Accuracy: Use a range of vocabulary and sentence structures for clarity, purpose and effect, combined with accurate spelling and punctuation. Sentence demarcation will be consistently secure and accurate with a wide range of punctuation, which is used with a high level of accuracy and provides impact to the writing. Use a full range of appropriate sentence forms for effect and use Standard English consistently and appropriately with a secure control of complex grammatical structures. Your essay must contain a high level of accuracy in spelling, including an extensive and ambitious use of vocabulary.

TIMINGS

In the AQA English Language GCSE Paper 1 and Paper 2 examinations there are 80 marks to aim for in 1 hour and 45 minutes (105 minutes). Please allocate the correct words per minute! Again, to re-iterate: The best approach is to spend 50 minutes on each question in Section B: - 40 minutes writing and 10 minutes making notes, planning and checking your final answer for basic corrections at the end of the examination.

If you have extra time allocated to you, just change the calculation to accommodate the extra time you have i.e., if you have 25% extra time (= 50 minutes writing per question = 12 words per minute) and if you have 50% extra time (= 1 hour writing per question = 10 words per minute), this also equals a 600-word essay. Please **move on from the set question as soon as you have reached or are coming towards your time limit**. This ensures that you have excellent coverage of your whole exam and therefore attain a very good mark.

Similar to all the principles in this book, **you must apply and follow the correct timings for each question and stick to them throughout your examination to get an A star (Grade 9) in your English Language examinations.** Without applying this principle in these examinations (and to a large extent all examinations) you cannot achieve the highest marks! *Apply all of the principles provided in this book to succeed.*

APPROXIMATE WORD COUNT PER QUESTION

Now that you know what is on each examination, how the assessment objectives are assessed and the time allocated for each type of question; we come to what would be considered the correct word count per mark for each question. **The primary principle though, is to spend the right amount of time on each question.**

In the answers in this book, I have provided the maximum word count theoretically possible for each answer which works out at **15 words per minute and per mark and this equals a 600-word essay**. If your answer has quality, this gives you the very best chance of obtaining the highest marks in your English Language exam. Obviously, it does not if you are waffling however (Please remember to answer the question set and to move on in the time allocated.).

I am aware that some students can write faster than others but all students should be able to write 10 words per minute and thus a 400-word essay (if they have not been allocated extra time). This is where conciseness is important in your writing.

My students and readers have applied all of the techniques of the Quality Control System™ I am providing you with; to gain A stars (Grade 9's) in their examinations. You can replicate them by following the advice in this book.

Thank you for purchasing this book and best wishes for your examinations!
Joseph

AUTHOR'S NOTE

This book will provide you with 12 crystal clear and accurate examples of 'A' star grade (Grade 9) AQA GCSE English Language Paper 2 Section B: Writing answers from the new syllabus and enables students to achieve the same grade in their upcoming examinations.

I teach both GCSE and A level English Language, English Literature, Sociology and Psychology and I am a qualified and experienced teacher and tutor of over 20 years standing. I teach, write and provide independent tuition in central and west London.

The resources in this book WILL help you to get an A star (Grade 9) in your GCSE English Language examinations, as they have done and will continue to do so, for my students.

Best wishes,

Joseph

ABOUT THE AUTHOR

I graduated from the Universities of Liverpool and Leeds and I obtained first class honours in my teacher training.

I have taught and provided private tuition for over 20 years up to university level. I also write academic resources for the Times Educational Supplement.

My tuition students, and now, my readers, have been fortunate enough to attain places to study at Oxford, Cambridge and Imperial College, London and other Russell Group Universities. The students have done very well in their examinations. I hope and know that my English Language, English Literature, Sociology and Psychology books can enable you to take the next step on your academic journey.

Printed in Great Britain
by Amazon

47079248R00031